GIFT OF REDEMPTION

Journey to Remember

Father Rick Tucker

GIFT OF REDEMPTION

Journey to Remember

Inner Healing through
the Stations of the Cross

Franciscan University Press
Franciscan University of Steubenville
Steubenville, OH 43952

Photographs: *The Crucifix of Brother Innocent*

The Crucifix of Brother Innocent hangs in the church of San Damiano in Assisi, Italy. The Crucifix was carved by Brother Innocent of Palermo in 1637 and depicts, with stark realism, the sufferings of the dying Jesus.

© 1990 Franciscan University Press. All rights reserved.

Photography: Angelo Lunghi, Assisi, Italy

Design: Art Mancuso

Published by:
Franciscan University Press
Franciscan University of Steubenville
Steubenville, OH 43952

Printed in the United States of America

ISBN: 0-940535-25-4

DEDICATION

Each one of us is asked to carry a cross in life. At times the cross is a very large one; at other times only a splinter from the cross causes suffering. When we are asked to carry that cross, the Lord often sends a "Simon" along to help us. There is a Simon in my life who has helped me to carry my cross, and who has given me the courage and confidence to write this book.

I dedicate this book to a brother who has been that Simon in my life. I dedicate this book of remembering to Mike Tragesser.

FOREWORD

Paul writes to us: "May I never boast of anything but the Cross of Jesus Christ, through it the world is crucified to me and I to the world." The Stations of the Cross blend for us the deepest loving compassion of Jesus, the total gift of redemption and forgiveness, and the exhortation to embrace the Cross and follow Jesus. Therefore, in the stations we have the healthiest approach to inner healing.

Michael Scanlan, T.O.R.

PREFACE

"To remember" means to think of an act or event again. We may remember a Christmas with family, or a special moment with a friend or loved one. When we remember the special words or gifts that were exchanged, we have the same warm feelings or perhaps the same pain they may have caused. The important part of remembering is that we were there once, and are there again.

These meditations on the cross are not meant to be a theological discourse on the death of Jesus. They are only meant to be a reflection that came from one person's meditation, and are now given to you to spark your meditation on the journey of the cross.

As you remember this journey, keep in mind that you are there once again; ask yourself how each step relates to your life. Just as Jesus made this journey of the cross, we must make it each day of our lives. Through these meditations, I pray that you may find a fresh anointing in your life; and a new, more powerful way to use any suffering you may encounter along the way.

Come now. Let us begin our journey.

Fr. Rick Tucker

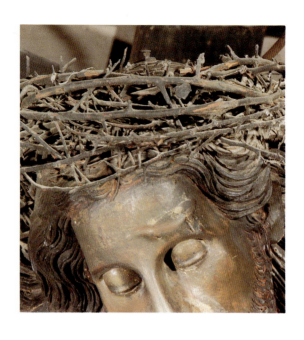

GIFT OF REDEMPTION - Father Rick Tucker

First Station

Jesus is condemned to death.
> Like a lamb led to slaughter,
> he went silently to his death.
> *Isaiah 53:7*

Jesus stands silently before his accusers, his hands bound, a crown of thorns on his head. The picture is one of humiliation—this helpless man enduring the jeers of the guards and the hate of the mob. The Roman authorities and Jewish religious leaders question him, insult him, accuse him. But he makes no reply. His refusal to defend himself infuriates them even more. They condemn him to death without cause.

MEDITATION

How often have I stood with my hands bound, my words being twisted, while false accusations were being made against me? Perhaps it was an argument with a relative or spouse, or a difference of opinion at work or some community service. I remember my indignation at the injustice of my treatment. How it hurt to be misunderstood, to be unjustly accused.

Then I must ask a more pain-filled question: how often have I stood in the shoes of the accuser? Whom have I bound up because of my gossip? Whom have I slandered by the rumors that I have spread over my morning coffee, lunch, supper, or phone calls?

I would rather see myself standing in the shoes of Jesus, but my heart tells me that I have often stood in the shoes of the accuser, judging others with hatred and unforgiveness. (Pause silently to reflect and remember.)

PRAYER

As I stand here, Lord, remembering your walk and all that happened to you, I must ask you to forgive me for the times I have stood in the shoes of the accuser. I have tied the hands of others by my false accusations, by my gossip. Heal the wounds I have inflicted on others by my actions or by my words.

Now, Lord, I forgive those who have wounded me. Heal my wounds on this journey of remembering.

Thank you, Lord.

Our Father, Hail Mary

14   GIFT OF REDEMPTION - Father Rick Tucker

Second Station

Jesus is made to bear his cross.
Whosoever would come with me,
must deny his own self,
take up his cross,
and begin to follow in my footsteps.
Matthew 16:24

Jesus is given the cross, the beam that he is to carry to the hill called Golgotha. He places his hands on it, and raises the beam to his shoulder. From his years of carpentry, he knows how to balance its weight and handle it with a minimum amount of effort. From the knotted surface and twisted grain, he knows what kind of wood it is, and how the tree it came from might have looked. His love for wood is part of his nature, and now he begins to know and love this special piece of wood. It is his own.

MEDITATION

For years, Jesus fashioned things from wood. Now, a wooden cross will be the tool to transform him into something much greater - the Redeemer. This was his destiny, his reason for coming into the world. He accepts the cross willingly, for he knows that no one else can carry the burden of sin that it represents. He chooses the cross, carries it with purpose, to do a task which only he can do.

Scripture says that I am to deny myself, pick up my cross and follow him. My cross is not made of wood; it is fashioned in the form of illness, children who have left the church, a spouse who has died and left me alone. My cross may also be in the form of alcoholism, cancer, or many other pains known only to me and to God.

Think for a moment of your cross. In your mind picture Jesus lifting your cross to your shoulder. Tell him that you will carry this cross. Tell him for whom you will offer this sacrifice.

Prayer

Lord, just as you lifted the beam to your shoulder, give me the gift of bearing my cross. Help me not to run from it, for I can bring healing and peace in a way that no one else can. Help me.

Our Father, Hail Mary

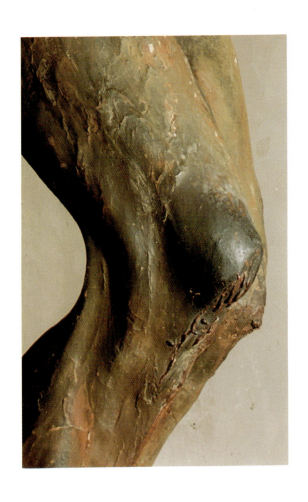

GIFT OF REDEMPTION - Father Rick Tucker

THIRD STATION

Jesus falls the first time.
> Show me the way in
> which I should walk,
> for to you I lift up my soul.
> *Psalms 143:8*

Jesus is carrying the cross through the streets of Jerusalem. Some take notice of him; others just see another condemned man going to his death. He has been up all night; he is tired and weak. Suddenly, he falls to the ground. The pain explodes in his body as he falls on open wounds. He lays there for a few moments and then forces himself to get up. His flesh is weak, but his spirit wants to go on with the journey.

MEDITATION

I have started to carry my cross with zeal. I have said, "Yes, Lord, I'll carry this cross for you," and then I have fallen. How often has my flesh grown weak and I have given in and have fallen under its weight? What did my heart say? Did I call to God, ask him for the strength to go on? He knows and reads my heart. That is the important part of the journey - the heart. It is from there, deep down, that the Spirit speaks to me. (Pause silently to reflect and remember.)

Prayer

Dear God, help me call on you when I fall. Help me find the strength to go on with this journey. Heal me of the fear that blocks me from yielding to your will.

Thank you, Lord.

Our Father, Hail Mary

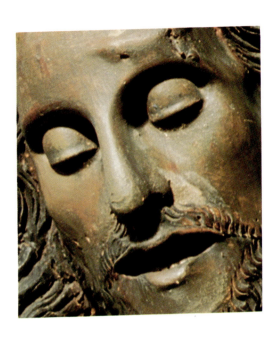

GIFT OF REDEMPTION - Father Rick Tucker

FOURTH STATION

**Jesus meets
his Sorrowful Mother.**
> Can a mother forget her infant,
> be without tenderness
> for the child of her womb?
> *Isaiah 49:15*

As he carries his cross, Jesus looks up and sees his mother. Like most sons, he is comforted just by her presence. He feels the pain that she is suffering for him, but he knows that she understands what he is doing. Yes, Mary has been beside Jesus from his conception until now, keeping all things close to her heart.

MEDITATION

What thoughts flood my mind as I stop and meditate on this encounter? Do my thoughts go back to a mother who was always there, who took care of me when I was ill or who sewed on my scout patches? If that is the mother I remember, then I must stop and give thanks. Do I recall instead a relationship that was broken? Was my mother one who, through no fault of her own, could not express her affection to me?

If my memory is flooded with a painful relationship, then I must ask for the healing power of Jesus. I accept his love for the times when my mother could not love me in the way I needed it.

Jesus, you see your mother as you walk this journey: a mother who loved you, who walked with you. As I walk this journey with you, memories rush to my mind. Some of them are pleasant; I give you praise and thanksgiving for them. There are others that bring me much pain. It is time for me to let go of the pain. (Pause and tell him those memories.)

PRAYER

Jesus, I ask you for the gift of peace in my heart, so that I may not fear what it may mean to let go of the pain. (Take a few moments to let the peace of Christ come into your heart.)

Lord, help me to forgive my mother for any pain I have experienced in our relationship. (Again, pause and let this forgiveness come into your heart.)

Now, Lord, I ask forgiveness for my part in the broken relationship: for the times I could have been more understanding, more forgiving, more loving. Thank you, Lord, for continuing to heal me. Help me to continue to be healed.

Our Father, Hail Mary

GIFT OF REDEMPTION - Father Rick Tucker

Fifth Station

Simon helps Jesus carry his cross.
>If anyone should press you
>into service for one mile,
>go with him two miles.
>*Matthew 5:41*

Simon was coming back from working in the fields. Although he was already tired from his own journey, he was made to carry the cross of Jesus. He was not asked because of compassion for Jesus, but because the soldiers wanted to keep things moving; to get the man up the hill to die.

MEDITATION

How many times have I been made to help carry another person's cross? Did I help because it would look good, or because I felt I couldn't say "No." Was there no love, no compassion in our actions - we just went along because there was no way out? Why is it that I don't reach out to help others to carry their crosses? What fear is in me, what old wound starts to ache and pulls me back? (Pause now and remember. Ask God to heal that pain, that wound.)

Who is it that has made my cross more difficult to carry? What was it that was said? What did they do or neglect to do that made my journey so difficult, my cross so heavy? (Picture them in your mind and speak your own words of forgiveness in your heart.)

You may say to yourself that you are

not able to forgive them. With God's grace, you can forgive. Ask for His help. Is there anyone who needs to forgive you? How often have you made another person's cross heavy because of your actions?

Prayer

Forgive me, Lord, for the times that I have acted out of duty and not out of real concern. Forgive me, Lord, for those times I resented being told to help others on their journey.

Lord, you have brought these people to my mind; that makes me remember that I must not only ask forgiveness, but I must give forgiveness to those who have hurt me. (Take a few moments to forgive.)

Thank you, Lord, for speaking to me as I stop at this station; continue to speak to me as we move on.

Our Father, Hail Mary

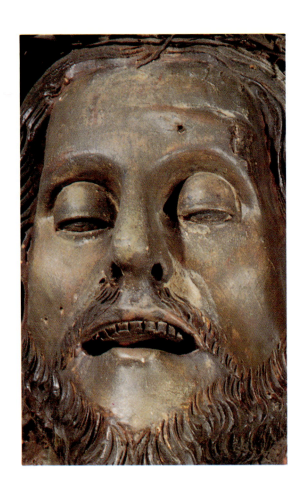

GIFT OF REDEMPTION - Father Rick Tucker

Sixth Station

Veronica wipes the face of Jesus.
Look toward me, and
have pity on me,
for I am alone and afflicted.
Psalms 25:16

As Jesus is walking on his journey, the perspiration running down his face mixes with the blood from his head wounds. Out of the crowd comes a holy woman, moved with pity for this man. She puts a cloth to his face to soothe the stinging wounds. Carefully she removes the blood-stained cloth. It is such a small gesture. She wishes that she could remove the injuries as well. But her act is not without value to Jesus. In a language deeper than words, his eyes express the heartfelt appreciation of her gift.

MEDITATION

Tradition tells us that when Veronica pulled the cloth away, the image of Jesus' face remained on it. What a priceless treasure this cloth would be, the face of Jesus traced with his own blood. Yet even more wonderful is the memory she treasured in her soul: a painting of gratitude on a canvas of compassion.

Remember the times you were tired and didn't think you could take another step on your journey? You were not tired because of a cross-beam of wood, but because of everyday life: tired because your family needs exceeded your means, worn out because you spent many hours taking children to ball practice or gymnastics class. You asked yourself, "Can I go another step?" Then a friend stepped out and wiped your face; not with a cloth, but with a cup of coffee, an encouraging word, or an hour to sit and listen to you. That word of thanks, that quiet moment of understanding - these are the cloths that soothe our wounds on the journey.

How often could I have stepped out with a cloth but said, "I don't have time," or, "Let someone else do it." (Pause to reflect, remember, and ask forgiveness.)

Prayer

Dear Lord, thank you for sending a "Veronica" to wipe my face on the journey. Heal me of any fear of being the one to step out and help, so that I can be a "Veronica" to other people.

Thank you, Lord.

Our Father, Hail Mary

GIFT OF REDEMPTION - Father Rick Tucker

SEVENTH STATION

Jesus falls the second time.
> Bear with one another;
> forgive whatever grievances
> you have against one another.
> *Colossians 3:13*

Jesus continues his climb up the hill of Calvary. The cross is heavy, but he carries it along with the help of Simon. Its weight is not the only hardship. The rough beam scrapes and tears his shoulder. Weakened by the pain of the cross and his wounds, he falls again.

MEDITATION

There are times when our steps falter under the weight of the cross; a cross of family problems, medical bills, or the loss of someone close. In these moments of great stress, friends and family gather and give support. With the help of a "Simon," we can go on.

There is another time we can fall under the cross: when we feel the pain of the splinters. We all have them - that person who rubs us the wrong way, the irritating habit of someone near us. (Pause and think about the person or thing that is the splinter in your life. Forgive them.)

Prayer

Father, once again I remember falling under the pain of the cross. Lord, I place the little splinters from my cross before you as I stand at this station. Heal me as I make this journey, so I may be a better instrument of your gospel each day.

Thank you, Lord.

Our Father, Hail Mary

GIFT OF REDEMPTION - Father Rick Tucker

EIGHTH STATION

Jesus meets the women of Jerusalem.
*Pour out your heart like water
in the presence of the Lord;
Lift up your hands to him
for the lives of your little ones.*
Lamentations 2:19

Jesus approaches the good women of Jerusalem. As they see Jesus, they weep, because of his pain and the injustice of his fate. Not seeking his own comfort, he tells them to weep not for him, but for themselves and their children. ''The days are coming when they will say, 'Happy the wombs that never bore and the breast that never nursed.' ''

MEDITATION

Jesus is saying to them and to us that if the day will come when the innocent will suffer, then what will the guilty have to endure? Just as the women of Jerusalem will have to suffer, so will the church have to suffer until she is cleansed of all impurity.

How often must we be told to repent of our sin and do penance for the world? Mary has brought us that same message again and again, and yet we do not listen. We hear, but do not listen, so we do not respond to the call.

What in my life do I need to weep for? What sin must I repent of and turn from? What acts of reparation can I make on behalf of the world? (Take time and place them before the Lord.)

PRAYER

Jesus, I place before you my own weaknesses. I will seek to confess them as soon as I can. I promise to do my act of penance for my sins and for the sins of the world. (Name what act of reparation you will do.)

Our Father, Hail Mary

GIFT OF REDEMPTION - Father Rick Tucker

NINTH STATION

Jesus falls a third time.
> Father, take this cup from me;
> yet not my will,
> but thine be done.
> *Luke 22:42*

Once again Jesus falls under the weight of his cross. He lays there for a while, panting with pain and exhaustion. After the other falls, he had to force his flesh to rise and go on. Now his spirit as well is tested to the limit. Part of him wants to give up the fight, to die here on the spot if the soldiers would allow it. But deep within himself he discovers another source of strength. Like the hard stones beneath him, there is a solid place at the very bottom of his soul. He braces himself on foundation of his free will, and makes a decision . . . to go on.

MEDITATION

I fall again! What do I do at this point? Do I lay there on the ground and say that I am unable to go on? Do I think such thoughts as, "If he had my failures he would not have been able to get up," or "What's the use; I have fallen too many times to try again."

Is my decision like that of Jesus? Do I decide to get up and go on? It isn't how many times we fall that is important. It is the fact that we say we are sorry and resolve to continue the journey.

Prayer

Dear Lord, once again I have fallen on the journey, and once again I come to my feet and continue on. Give me the fight of perseverence rather than discouragement. Help me develop the attitude of victory rather than defeat.

Thank you, Lord.

Our Father, Hail Mary

GIFT OF REDEMPTION - Father Rick Tucker

Tenth Station

Jesus is stripped of his clothes.
Naked I came forth from my mother's womb, and naked shall I go back again.
Job 1:21

As was the practice of the Romans, Jesus is stripped of his garments. It is a great humiliation in the Jewish culture, to have one's nakedness exposed in full public view. Jesus yields himself to the insult, refusing even to hold on to pride in the submission to his fate. By his nakedness he proclaims his oneness with all the poor, the naked, the sick and the dying, whom he has come to save.

MEDITATION

In a different way I must be stripped of my garments. Yes, I must come to the point where I can take off my garments and stand before the Lord; garments such as pride that makes me refuse to admit my weakness, those masks I wear so that people will not know who I really am, and so they will not be able to touch me deep in my center.

Yes, I must learn to come to Jesus Christ not as I wish to be, but as I am now. It is the only way that I can be changed to become like him.

Prayer

Father, show me the fear that keeps me from standing before you just as I am. Reveal to me the anything that makes me hide from you. (Take some time and let the Lord show you your fears.)

Now, Lord, to the extent that I am able, I give this fear to you. I stand before you stripped, as vulnerable to you as I can be at this time.

Thank you for starting to heal me.

Our Father, Hail Mary

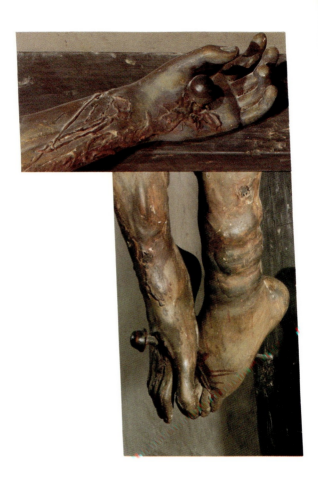

Eleventh Station

Jesus is nailed to the cross.
Therefore I am content with weakness,
with mistreatment, with distress,
with persecutions and difficulties
for the sake of Christ, for when I am
powerless, it is then that I am strong.
2 Corinthians 12:10

The cross is dropped on the ground and Jesus is thrown onto the hard beam. As the nails enter the wrists, the tendons pull the fingers into cruel contortions. The severed nerves shoot bolts of fire through both arms. The nail is driven through the feet, making the torture complete. Now every part of his body is racked with an agony that cannot be described.

MEDITATION

Sometimes we would like to think that we need not remember the death of Jesus - we need only look at the resurrection. Yet, am I better than the master? Should I expect a life free from pain and suffering? No! The work of salvation must go on, and my pain can be offered for the good of myself and others. Saint Paul tells us to offer prayers and petitions of every sort. Daily pain and suffering can be that prayer.

How do I deal with the "nails" that come into my life? Do I become angry? Do I feel that God has abandoned me? Or do I turn to Him and ask for healing if it is His will? If I am not healed, do I offer up my nails for the glory of God and the good of all people? (Pause and place your nails before him.)

PRAYER

Lord, when those days or weeks or even "that year" comes into my life, help me to remember what you went through in your life. Help me to remember to offer up hard times to you. Thank you for the strength to bear the nails in my life.

Our Father, Hail Mary

54   GIFT OF REDEMPTION - Father Rick Tucker

Twelfth Station

Jesus dies on the Cross.
   Father, I put my life in your hands.
      Psalms 31:6

Jesus has hung on the cross for three hours, fighting to stay alive. The weight of his body prevents him from exhaling, and he would soon die of asphyxiation. Pushing against the nails in his feet, he lifts himself up to take another breath. He purchases another minute of life with a ransom of pain. But at last, the struggle must end; he tries to raise himself, but his legs do not have the strength. Knowing that the end has come, he cries out his last breath: "Father, into your hands I commend my spirit."

MEDITATION

There are many types of death we can experience: our own body, the death of a loved one, and death to self. Death to myself is very difficult, because I must have faith in God to put my life into His hands. In a word, this kind of death is abandonment.

What part of me struggles against my putting my life in God's hands? (Think about whatever causes you to struggle.)

Say with Jesus His prayer of abandonment, substituting for the word "spirit" the part of yourself that you need to give him: "Father, into your hands I commend my . . ."

Prayer

Father, it is hard to abandon myself to you, to walk this journey and to allow myself to go to the cross; and yet it must be. Give me the grace to take that next step into your hands.

Thank you, Lord.

Our Father, Hail Mary

THIRTEENTH STATION

The body of Jesus is taken down from the Cross.

And you yourself shall be pierced with a sword - so that the thoughts of many hearts shall be laid bare.
Luke 2:35

Mary has stood quietly by, pondering all things in her heart. Now she has one more pain to endure. Jesus is taken down from the cross. His wet, bloody body is placed in her arms. She gave life to this body; now it is still and dead. Mary weeps as another sword of grief pierces her soul.

MEDITATION

Only a parent who has lost a son or daughter can understand the torment that Mary felt that afternoon. You may have been asked to endure the loss of your child because of war, an accident, illness, miscarriage, or suicide. If you have experienced this anguish, you know how deep was the ache she felt.

How often have you longed to cry out to someone about this pain, yet could not find anyone who would understand? Mary, the mother of Jesus - and yes, your mother - understands the pain. See Mary in your mind. Her arms are opened to you. Speak to her from your heart and receive your comfort from her. (Pause now and speak with your mother. Let her bring comfort to you.)

If you have not experienced such pain, pray for those who have had to bear this cross.

Prayer

Mary, my mother, hold me in your arms now as you held your helpless son. Pray with me that the pain I feel will be healed. Comfort me in the grief I still feel over my loss. Help me to let go, to release my child into God's hands.

Our Father, Hail Mary

GIFT OF REDEMPTION - Father Rick Tucker

FOURTEENTH STATION

Jesus is laid in the tomb.
> If we have died with Christ,
> we believe that we are
> also to live with him.
> *Romans 6:8*

The body of Jesus is taken to the tomb. Reverently the body is wrapped in the shroud and laid to rest. The mourners take one last look and then leave the tomb in silence. The entrance is sealed with a large stone. The sun is setting; the Sabbath Day is at hand. For now, all has been done that can be done. It is time to find rest for the body and peace of mind.

MEDITATION

Just as the body of Jesus was laid in the tomb, there are things that you have discovered on this journey that needs to be put to rest. Hidden wounds have been revealed so that healing may begin. Old wounds have been touched so that healing may be completed. The healing process will continue on its own. But for now, these hurts need to be set aside so that life and strength may be renewed. Pause now and name the person, place or event that God has asked you to release.

Picture in your mind the open entrance of the tomb. You walk inside and down a few steps. There stands Jesus, his arms outstretched to receive whatever you need to leave behind. He takes it from you and places it on the stone slab. Then he takes your hand

and leads you back up the steps and outside. He rolls a large stone across the opening; as the stone settles into place, you feel the weight of your burden lifted. The two of you walk away to continue your journey of life together.

PRAYER

Jesus, I thank you for the gift of this journey. Thank you for allowing me to experience your healing power, and for helping me to release so many things to you. On those days when I want to open the tomb and take them back, give me the grace to leave them with you. As I continue my journey, please lead me to other areas of my life that need to be healed. Allow me to leave behind in the tomb whatever burdens are no longer needed.

Our Father, Hail Mary

Go Now . . .

Remember, I will be with you always,
even unto the ends of the world.
Matthew 28:20

You have walked a journey of remembering. Now you must return to your everyday life - back to the office, factory, school or home. You will once again face the daily crosses that will come your way, but the experience will be far different from before because of the journey you have just taken. In each situation, you will remember the people, places, and events that you have met on this walk. Now you know what to do with each cross you find along the way.

Go now and continue your journey. Remember where you have been and trust in the journey ahead.

Come, Lord Jesus; walk with me.

Our Father, Hail Mary